Martin Koch

Better Gray in Print on Demand

How to improve grayscale appearance
in toner based, 600 dots per inch printing

© 2006, Verlag Martin Koch, Hartbergerstrasse 22a, 8200 Gleisdorf, Austria

ISBN-13: 978-3-901314-13-1
ISBN-10: 3-901314-13-X

Preface

I publish guitar building books with a lot of photos in it (see www.buildyourguitar.com) and I use Lightning Source Inc. an US and UK based print on demand company for printing my English books. Unfortunately grayscale reproduction leaves much to be desired in 600 dpi laser printing so using grayscale images is not recommended in print on demand. But grayscale is everywhere be it photos or screenshots. Sometimes as a publisher you have no choice. This book examines some ways to improve the appearance of gray in a print on demand book.

Contents

Open source alternatives to Adobe programs

I use Photoshop throughout this book. It is a powerful image editor and the de facto standard. Although some features I use are only available in Photoshop CS2 or higher any Photoshop version has the basic functionality needed. If you don't need the newest version take a look at eBay.

An open source alternative to Photoshop is Gimp (www.gimp.org). An open source alternative to Adobe Illustrator is Inkscape (www.inkscape.org) and an open source alternative to InDesign is Scribus (www.scribus.net). All this free alternatives are available for Windows and Mac OS X and some other operating systems.

I cannot advise an alternative to Adobe Acrobat Professional though. This software is highly recommended for producing PDF files.

About Lightning Source

Lightning Source (www.lightningsource.com) is one of the world's largest print on demand companies with a huge output each day. While there are other print on demand companies Lightning source is unique because it is a division of Ingram publishing. All Lightning Source print on demand books can be ordered in American or Canadian book shops and from the world's largest bookstore Amazon (amazon.com, amazon.ca, amazon.fr and amazon.co.jp). There's also a branch in United Kingdom for supplying the UK bookmarket via Bertram and also amazon.co.uk.

Lightning Source doesn't work directly with individual authors. They work with publishers and they request print ready files. Everything must be prepared by the publisher. Individual authors are referred to publishing partners which then use Lightning Source printing facilities.

Lightning Source does everything for you

All bookstore and online orders are handled by Lightning Source. They print, package and ship each individual order. There are no inventory costs at all. You just pay for printing and shipping of books that got actually sold. If you sell your book(s) exclusively via Lightning Source's infrastructure all you have to do is to wait for your monthly publisher compensation check to arrive (if any books where ordered this month of course). Printing and shipping costs get automatically subtracted so you don't even have to pay a bill.

Publisher compensation

You determine the price of your book and the discount you are willing to offer to book stores. Your monthly publisher compensation is the book price minus the discount minus the printing costs. Publisher compensation is paid three month later i.e. you get the check for your January publisher compensation in April. Publisher compensation reports are sent to you every month by email and can also be viewed at lightningsource.com.

Book returns

If you allow your book to be returned by the customer any returns will also be subtracted from your publisher compensation. You decide if a book is returnable or not. Usually books that are returnable are ordered more willingly by book stores. If your book has good content you don't have to fear many returns. If books are returnable you can choose whether returned copies get destroyed by Lightning Source or are sent to you at a charge.

Selling books yourself

You can also order books for personal distribution. This orders are called short run orders and printing and shipping costs will be billed to you.

If you want Lightning Source even ships short run orders directly to your customer. Short run orders can be placed and controlled via their web interface from any computer with internet connection around the world. Bills are paid by credit card. Delivery of short run orders can conveniently be followed by an UPS tracking number. There's no minimum order quantity, you can order one book at a time. Printing costs are somewhat lower if you order 100 books and even lower for orders of 200 and more. But if you can sell this many in short time you could also use conventional offset printing of 1000 copies with much lower printing costs per copy and better printing quality. There will still be the problem of getting into the book market though.

What's used for print on demand?

Print on demand is a toner based printing process. Very much like your desktop laser printer but at a much larger scale. The pages of a whole book are printed, cut and bound in very short time. Every single book is printed on demand i.e. only when it is ordered.

Quote from an IBM business case study:
"Originally, Lightning Source installed a black-and-white 600 dot-per-inch (dpi) IBM Infoprint 4000 printer, which printed 464 impressions per minute (ipm).
However, the company has upgraded systems several times in recent years to take advantage of technology advances. The most recent upgrade, which occurred in April 2005, quadrupled the capacity of the Lightning Source print floor. Lightning Source now has eight black-and-white print lines in its U.S. location, including three IBM Infoprint 4100 HD1/HD2 systems and five IBM 4100 w/HD4 systems. Lightning Source also uses two IBM Infoprint 4100 HD1/HD2 printers in its U.K. location. The Infoprint 4100 printers provide an economical continuous-forms printing solution."

Lightning Source workhorse: The IBM Infoprint 4100

600 dots per inch

The 600 dots per inch (dpi) of current print on demand machines is a good compromise between type and line art quality and storage space usage. In fact the inexperienced customer will hardly notice a quality difference between a text printed with 600 dpi or an offset press.

> **A 600 dpi printer puts a dot on paper every 1/600th of an inch. This is quite fine.**
>
> **1 / 600 = 0.0017 inch**
> **or 0.04 mm**

This one inch square is filled with 600 x 600 = 360,000 black dots

180,000 toner dots got wasted to fill this pointless half inch square.

This 1 pt line uses up about 8.3 x 600 = 4980 black printer dots per inch (1 pt = 1/72 inch)

The 0.25 pt line just above this text is built up by approximately two rows of printer dots. Avoid finer lines than this in print on demand because lines below 0.25 pt may not print reliable.

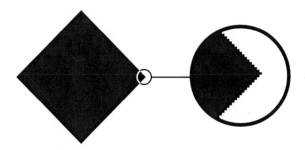

Resolution becomes an issue when edges are angled. But as the square above and also the black type of this text proofs you will hardly notice any steps at 600 dpi.

Line art performs well in print on demand

Line art is black and white only graphics. You can use software to make it or use a scanner to bring it into the computer. Line art is very small in file size because only 1-bit has to be stored for each pixel. If possible prepare line art in the original size because any resizing will degrade the picture quality. If you have to resize line art then do it in Photoshop using the IMAGE > IMAGE SIZE... dialog. If it is available in your Photoshop version then use *Resample Image: Bicubic sharper* if you scale it down or *Resample Image: Bicubic Smoother* if you make it bigger. Always set the resolution to the printer resolution. In our case "600 pixels/inch".

Line art like me shouldn't be resized in the layout program. I look best at 100% size.

The images shown on this page and the facing page are line art. Each pixel is either black or white. The 100% size is determined by the image height and width in pixels and the 600 dpi resolution.

100%

Manga and Comics artists have turned the limitations of low resolution, black and white printing into an art of its own. Print on Demand should be great for this type of publishing.

Under water scene drawn by my son Markus. Scanned into Photoshop as a grayscale image with 600 ppi. Converted to a bitmap using

IMAGE > ADJUSTMENTS > IMAGE SIZE
IMAGE > ADJUSTMENTS > THRESHOLD
IMAGE > MODE > BITMAP > 50% THRESHOLD
FILE > SAVE AS > BMP

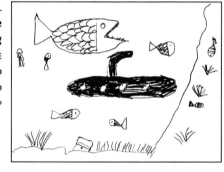

Black vector art and type perform well in print on demand

Vector art are mathematically described lines and shapes. It can be scaled at any time and will always print with the full printer resolution no matter what size. If you draw a line or a frame in your layout program it's vector art.

Type is a specific form of vector graphics.

Type can be scaled

at any time without degrading printing quality. Black type always prints with the full printer resolution no matter what size.

Different line weights and how they print
One point equals 1/72 inch. Lines below 0.25 point should be avoided.

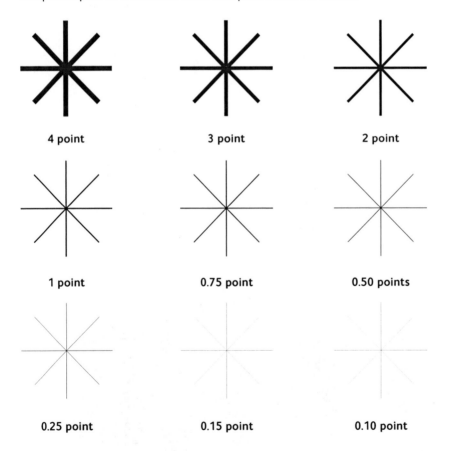

4 point	3 point	2 point
1 point	0.75 point	0.50 points
0.25 point	0.15 point	0.10 point

100% size as drawn
in Illustrator

Line width:
0.75 pt and 1.2 pt

The small and the large line drawings above are
resized copies of the middle vector art. Note that
the line weight also gets scaled.

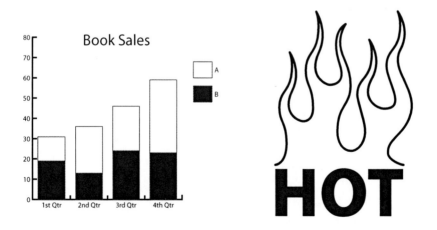

How a laser printer prints gray

A monochrome laser printer cartridge contains only black toner. It prints only black. White comes from the paper and any gray has to be simulated by fooling the eye. If you look at the area below from a distance you'll see gray although only black and white was used.

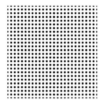

The one inch square above shows a pattern of black dots arranged on a grid at a distance of 0.04 inch. Each row of dots is lined up therefore we can say that the gray above is simulated by 1 / 0.04 = 25 lines per inch (lpi).

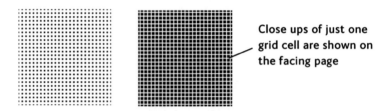

Close ups of just one grid cell are shown on the facing page

By decreasing or increasing the darkness within each grid cell a lighter or a darker gray can be simulated. Note that the centre line distance of all dot rows stays the same. The grid or line screen in the examples above is always 25 lpi.

To make a line screen less visible it is usually applied at an angle of 45 degrees

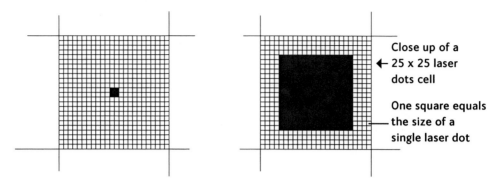

Close up of a
← 25 x 25 laser
dots cell

One square equals
the size of a
single laser dot

Unfortunately a laser printer can only print one single dot size. Varying dot sizes must be simulated by grouping several laser dots together. What you see above is just one cell of the previous 25 lpi grid. To completely fill one of this 0.04 inch squares a 600 dpi printer needs 24 x 24 laser dots (600 x 0.04 = 24). A completely filled grid appears as 100% gray (black). This 24 x 24 laser dots can now be used to simulate 577 different shades of gray (pure white plus 576 dot patterns from just one dot to a fully filled grid cell).

577 shades of gray are more you'll ever need so let's make the grid finer to get halftone dots that can hardly be noticed. A four times finer screen of 100 lpi would be good. But look, the cell size is now only 1/100 of an inch. Just 6 x 6 laser dots fit into this smaller halftone cell. Suddenly only 36 shades of gray plus pure white can be simulated. That's poor. You have to find a good compromise which for a 600 dpi printer can be 85 lpi. The halftone screen isn't too visible and there are 50 (49 + 1) possible shades of gray.

> **# of gray values = (printer dpi / screen lpi)² + 1**
> E.g. a 85 lpi screen printed on a 600 dpi printer
> can simulate about 50 shades of gray:
> 600 / 85 = 7.06
> 7.06 x 7.06 = 49.48
> 49.48 + 1 = 50.48

Laser printer resolution and recommended line screens		
Printer dpi	Recommended lpi	# of gray values
300	50	37
600	85	50
1200	106	128

The problem with gray in print on demand

The problem with gray in 600 dpi print on demand is that all gray is screened with the same coarse line screen. As explained later grayscale photos require a line screen below 90 lpi to look acceptable. If you have photos in your book this coarse line screen is also applied to gray vector art because the Raster Image Processor (RIP) of the printer doesn't differentiate between grayscale photos and gray in vector art. Gray is gray and it is screened with the default line screen. If you write a book on some software and all gray you have in your book is in screenshot images then you could set a finer line screen for the entire book (I don't think that this is possible with Lightning Source though because they always use a 85 lpi line screen).

The left image is an 8-bit grayscale photo and the right one is a box filled with gray. The box is vector art and was drawn in the layout program. As you can see both grays got screened by the same line screen. In therory you can avoid this by prescreening gray vector art with a finer line screen as shown below.

The gray box above was made with Photoshop. First I started a new document in 8-bit *Grayscale Mode* with the dimensions of the box and a resolution of 600 ppi. Then I filled the document with gray and converted it into *Bitmap Mode* using IMAGE > MODE > BITMAP with the following settings: *Halftone Screen - 600 ppi - 100 lpi - 45° - round dot*. This conversion prescreened the gray with a fine 100 lines per inch screen. The box above is independent from the printers screening setting because it is offered to the Raster Image Processor as line art and was printed as such. **I don't understand why but 100 lpi prescreened uniform gray areas appeared with stripes in a previous proof copy of this book although they printed very well on my laser printer.** The method worked for screenshots though and I used this prescreening technique for all screenshots in this book. Because there are also grayscale photos in this book that require 85 lpi this was the only way to make sure that the gray in the screenshots doesn't look coarse.

On the next pages you can take a detailed look at such prescreened bitmaps.

A closer look at prescreened gray

Above:
50% and 25% gray after converting to Photoshops *Bitmap Mode* using a
600 ppi / 50 lpi, 45° round dot halftone screen.

Below:
Extreme zoom into the bitmap data of the gray area above (you see a transition
area from 50% to 25% gray). The coarse screen can simulate 12 x 12 = 144 shades
of gray on a 600 dpi printer. When viewed at 100% the average impression of all
pixels is gray.

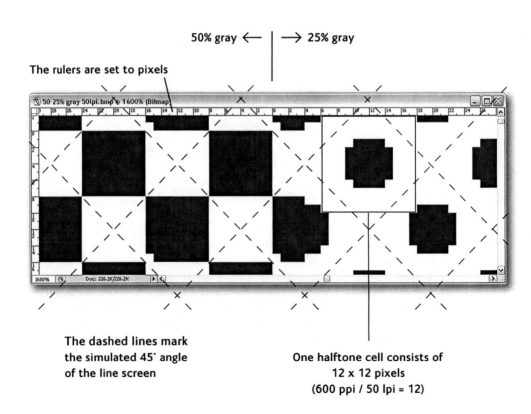

50% gray ⟵ | ⟶ 25% gray

The rulers are set to pixels

50 25% gray 50lpi.bmp @ 1600% (Bitmap)

1600%   Doc: 226.2K/226.2K

The dashed lines mark
the simulated 45° angle
of the line screen

One halftone cell consists of
12 x 12 pixels
(600 ppi / 50 lpi = 12)

I don't understand why but the prescreened 50% gray area below appeared with stripes in a previous proof copy of this book although it printed very well on my laser printer.

Above:
50% and 25% gray after converting to Photoshops Bitmap mode using a
600 ppi / 100 lpi, 45° round dot halftone screen.

Below:
Detail view of the bitmap data for the gray area above. The relatively fine screen can simulate only 6 x 6 = 36 shades of gray on a 600 dpi printer. When viewed at 100% the average impression of all pixels is gray.

One halftone cell consists of
6 x 6 pixels (600 ppi / 100 lpi = 6)

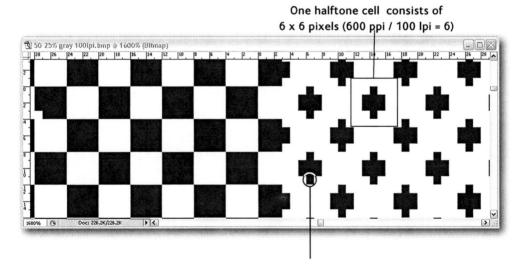

Note that one pixel equals one printer dot. The simulation of 25% gray shows details as fine as a single printer dot!

Recommended values of gray

If you use gray shades in your text or art work limit it to 20% steps. The lightest gray should have a value of no less then 20%. This limits the possible number of shades to four as shown below. I also added the corresponding RGB values in a short form i.e. RGB=204 should read R=204, G=204, B=204 for example.

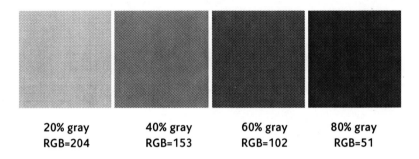

| 20% gray | 40% gray | 60% gray | 80% gray |
| RGB=204 | RGB=153 | RGB=102 | RGB=51 |

The same gray values as above prescreened with 600 ppi / 100 lpi. I don't understand why but the gray squares appeared with stripes in a previous proof copy of this book although they printed very well on my laser printer.

Pre-screened with 600 ppi / 150 lpi. This screen simulates 18 shades of gray. But it prints bad because 150 lpi is too fine for a 600 dpi printer.

Things to avoid in print on demand

Placing text on gray background is one of the things to avoid in print on demand publishing. Because of the coarse screen it doesn't look good and text is difficult to read.

Placing small text on gray background is one of the things to avoid in print on demand publishing. It doesn't look good and text is difficult to read.

40% gray background

60% gray background

20% gray background

20% gray background prescreened with 100 lpi

60% gray background prescreened with 100 lpi

80% gray background prescreened with 100 lpi

100% gray (black) background

10 point bold text with 14 point leading. White text on black background can also be problematic because toner based printing is not able to print uniform areas of black reliable. Very often a washed-out look is the result.

10 point regular text with 14 point leading. White text on black background can also be problematic because toner based printing is not able to print uniform areas of black. Very often a washed-out look is the result. Increase the leading to make the white text more readable.

Bold 10 point text on a 10% gray background looks quite good.

Bold 10 point text on a 20% gray background also looks acceptable.

10 pt text placed on a frame filled with 10% gray. The 1-bit bitmap background was pre-screened in Photoshop at 100 lpi, 45° using a round dot.

SQUARE DOT BACKGROUND

10 pt text placed on a frame filled with 10% gray. The 1-bit bitmap background was pre-screened in Photoshop at 100 lpi, 45° using a square dot.

10 pt text placed on a frame filled with 20% gray. The 1-bit bitmap background was pre-screened in Photoshop at 100 lpi, 45° using a round dot.

The background was prepared in Photoshop as large as the book page and placed into this frame. This text was then placed in an extra frame on top of it.

SQUARE DOT BACKGROUND

10 pt text placed on a frame filled with 20% gray. The 1-bit bitmap background was pre-screened in Photoshop at 100 lpi, 45° using a square dot.

BLACK
GRAY

GRAY TYPE GETS SCREENED

Small gray type gets screened and looks terrible.
Small gray type gets screened and looks terrible.
Small gray type gets screened and looks terrible.
Small gray type gets screened and looks terrible.

THIS TYPE IS 99% BLACK
WILL IT GET SCREENED?

This is 20% gray type

This is 40% gray type

This is 60% gray type

This is 20% gray type

This is 40% gray type

This is 60% gray type

The headlines above are type.

This is 20% gray type

This is 40% gray type

This is 60% gray type

This is 20% gray type

This is 40% gray type

This is 60% gray type

The headlines above are 1-bit bitmap line art pre-screened in Photoshop with a 100 lpi line screen. I wanted to say that if you really can't live without gray headlines this may be a way to go. But after seeing the result printed on my laser printer I would prefer type. Photoshop does some mean things to type when it converts it to pixels.

Anyway you could still add such a bitmap headline to the table of contents by putting an additional invisible headline on the page. Fill the headline type with white to hide it or if you use InDesign you can put the headline on an invisible layer and then check *Include Text on Invisible Layers* when generating the table of contents.

How to prepare screenshots for print on demand

Taking the screenshot
Most of the time it is necessary to process screenshots in Photoshop so copying the screenshot right to the *Clipboard* memory is the fastest method.
There is dedicated screenshot software available but Windows and Mac OS X also offer this functionality. Just memorize the following keyboard shortcuts it may be all you ever need:
In **Windows** hitting the PRINT SCREEN key in the upper right area of your keyboard takes a screenshot of the entire screen and copies it to the *Clipboard* memory.
Pressing ALT + PRINT SCREEN does the same with the active window.
In **Mac OS X** SHIFT + CONTROL +COMMAND + 4 will give you a cross hair to drag and copies the capture into the *Clipboard* memory.

Processing the screenshot in Photoshop
Paste the screenshot. Open a new Photoshop document (FILE > NEW). The new document dialog in Photoshop will automatically show the dimensions of the screenshot in the *Clipboard* memory. Press OK and paste the screenshot into the new document (EDIT > PASTE). It will fit like a glove. In Windows STRG+N, ENTER, STRG+V and in Mac OS X COMMAND+N, ENTER, COMMAND+V does the same thing but much faster.

Convert to *Grayscale Mode*. After pasting the screenshot convert it to *Grayscale Mode* (IMAGE > MODE > GRAYSCALE).

Resize the screenshot: Resize it to 600 dpi and the dimensions needed. This will almost always require an enlargement so use *Resample Image: Bicubic Smoother* if available.

Apply sharpening. Apply sharpening for 100 lpi, uncoated paper. I used nik Sharpener Pro for this.

Get rid of the gray corners. Mac OS X and modern Microsoft Windows versions have windows with round top corners. Because a screenshot is always square there may be ugly background pixels at the top corners. Unless you can place the Window on a white background these corners must be cleaned up. If both corners have the same color SELECT > COLOR RANGE and clicking on the gray of one of the corners will help. The other corner should get selected automatically but also some areas within the Window that are the same shade of gray. Hit OK and hold down the ALT key while selecting everything below the round corners with the rectangular marquee tool. Holding the ALT key will show a minus sign in the selection cursor which means that this selection gets subtracted from the previous one. When only the gray in the two top corners remains selected make sure that the background color in the tool palette is set to white. Press the BACKSPACE key to fill the selection with white. To avoid this procedure you could also switch to the classic Windows look in *Display Preferences* window before taking the screenshot. There's no such option for Mac OS X.
Removing gray corners in a prescreened screenshot is a breeze: zoom in and use the eraser tool set to a one pixel size to erase black corner pixels.
Another option to remove round corners is to cut off the top of the window.

Options to deal with the shades of gray in a screenshot.
1) Get rid of all gray by converting the screenshot into *Bitmap Mode* (IMAGE > MODE > BITMAP)
Use a *Threshold* of 50% to turn any gray into white. Redo (EDIT > REDO) and increase the *Threshold* percentage if gray turns to black. The resulting look reminds of old days when computers where young and may not be what you want.
2) Use the screenshot as is and let it screen by the RIP (see examples below).
3) Prescreen the screenshot. Since there are just a few shades of gray you can use a finer screen. IMAGE > MODE > BITMAP - Halftone screen - 600 ppi -100 lpi - 45˚ - round dot should be fine with 37 possible shades of gray. I've chosen this option for all screenshots in this book except for the one below and the ones on the next two pages.

Add a drop shadow. A drop shadow makes the screenshot stand out of the page nicely. I applied the drop shadows in InDesign using the default setting of 75% opacity. Because white in bitmaps is transparent everything inside the screenshot also dropped a shadow. I had to fill the image place holder frames with a white background color to get rid of this extra shadow.

Want to know this www.apple.com/pro/tips "secret"?
In Mac OS X Control-Command-Shift-3 copies an entire screen to the Clipboard Memory while Control-Command-Shift-4 gives you a cross hair cursor so you can choose in advance which area of the screen you want to capture.

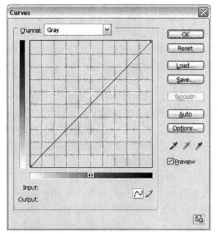

Placed as 300 ppi, 8-bit grayscale image

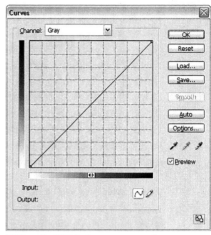

600 ppi- 100 lpi prescreened

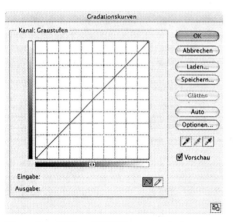

Placed as 300 ppi, 8-bit grayscale image

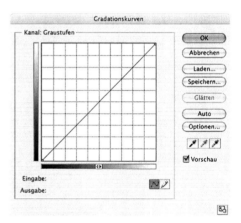

600 ppi -100 lpi prescreened

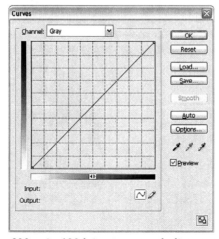

600 ppi - 100 lpi prescreened - line screen

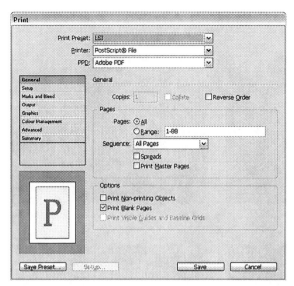

Placed as 300 ppi, 8-bit grayscale image

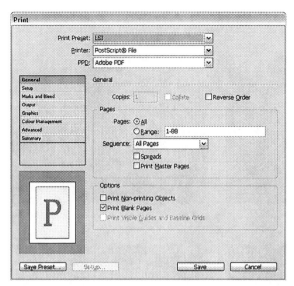

600 ppi -100 lpi prescreened

How line screens affect grayscale appearance

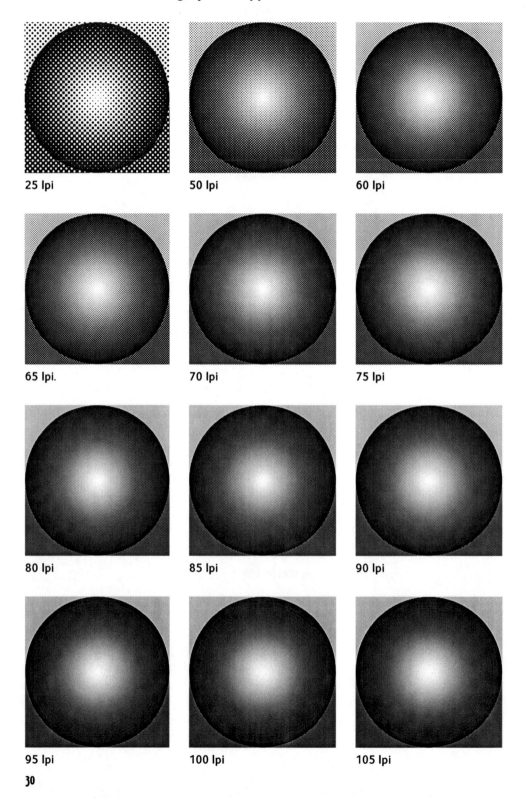

25 lpi

50 lpi

60 lpi

65 lpi.

70 lpi

75 lpi

80 lpi

85 lpi

90 lpi

95 lpi

100 lpi

105 lpi

Facing page:
Note how the black area at the perimeter grows with lesser available shades of gray.
The most beautiful ball is the one with 25 lpi... when viewed from an 8 feet distance!

This page:
Different line screens applied to an 8-bit grayscale gradient with 256 shades of gray from pure black on top to pure white on bottom. Steps appear in the gradients above 60 lpi when the number of possible grays gets too low. You can also see the loss of gray shades in the increasing length of the black or white ends of the gradient strips.

Line screen (lpi)	25	50	60	75	85	100	125	150
Possible shades of gray	577	145	101	65	50	36	24	17

How many shades of gray can we see?

We are capable of seeing any shade of gray but there is a limit in the number of shades our eyes can discriminate. We need a certain difference in brightness of the gray to see two different grays close to each other. Most humans need a 1% change in brightness to discriminate between two shades of gray. That would be about 100 different shades of gray under ideal viewing conditions. In practise because of not so ideal lighting conditions and other factors it's about 64 shades of gray or more. That's why the examples on the facing page can pass as grayscale image even with this low number of possible grays. If only the line screen could be finer.

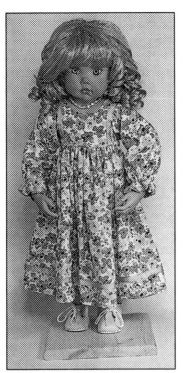

65 lpi - 85 shades of gray

75 lpi - 65 shades of gray

85 lpi - 50 shades of gray

Porcelain puppet
wearing a dress
made by my mother.

Different types of screen dot shapes

The standard halftone dot is round but by choosing another dot type you can make an image appear different as shown on the facing page. The source for the examples on the facing page was an 8-bit grayscale photo with sharpening applied for 85 lines per inch. Using other dot shapes needs much experimenting and I suggest to stick with the standard round dot for photo realistic grayscale images.

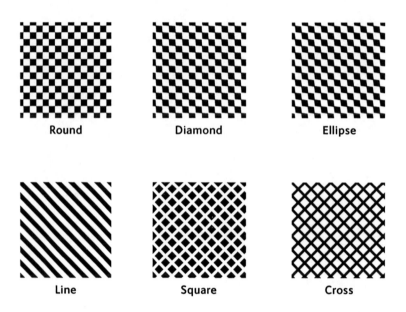

Round	Diamond	Ellipse

Line	Square	Cross

Above: 50% gray simulated by a 10 lines per inch screen with different dot shapes

Facing page: grayscale images with a 85 lpi line screen and different dot shapes.

Round

Diamond

Ellipse

Line

Square

Cross

Special effect screens

Screens don't necessarily need to have lines. Gray can also be simulated by randomly arranged tiny pixel patterns. Such random screens are also known as frequency modulated screens, FM screens, stochastic screens, diffusion dither screens or mezzotints. The diffusion dither examples on this page where made in Photoshop. A 600 ppi grayscale image was converted into *Bitmap Mode* using IMAGE > MODE > BITMAP as shown in the screenshot below.

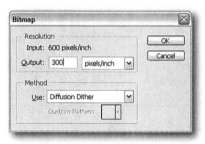

Mezzotints are patterns of irregular, worm-like shapes. They can be made in Photoshop using FILTER > PIXELATE > MEZZOTINT or with more control and much better results with special Photoshop plugins like the Andromeda Screens Filter (www.andromeda.com). Mezzograms are Andromedas term for a Mezzotint applied to an extremely sharpened image and Mezzoblends are blends between different screens.

Close up of special effect screen patterns

**Photoshop
Diffusion Dither**

**Photoshop
Mezzotint Filter**

**Andromeda Screens
Mezzotint**

Photoshop
300 ppi Diffusion Dither

Photoshop
200 ppi Diffusion Dither

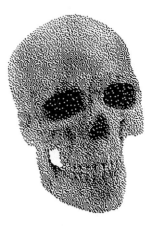

Photoshop
100 ppi Diffusion Dither

Andromeda Screens
100 worms/inch Mezzotint

Andromeda Screens
100 worms/inch Mezzogram

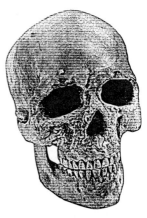

Andromeda Screens
Straight lines Mezzoblend

Ways to optimize grayscale pictures for print on demand

Start with correctly exposed photographs

Every time you have to correct an under- or overexposed image in Photoshop you loose image data because you have to spread the tonal values apart. Better start with a correctly exposed image that only needs small adjustments so most of the original image data is preserved.

I never feeled confident about correctly exposing my photographs until a book with the very long title *The Confused Photographer's Guide to Photographic Exposure and the Simplified Zone System* by Bahman Farzad. I remembered that I had already read about this in other books but it was this book that made me understanding the simple concept.

If you have ever wondered how your camera determines exposure values do a quick experiment. You need a uniform white, a uniform black and a uniform middle gray area. The size is not relevant just hold your camera in front of each of the colored areas so that all you see in the viewfinder is the color. There is also no need for correct focus. Take a photograph of each color and let the camera decide how to exposure each one by using its auto exposure mode. When you take a look at the result (your digital cameras monitor will be fine for this) you will see that every single picture is gray.

Your cameras exposure system is not smart it is designed to always adjust exposure so that the average tone of any scene in the viewfinder equals 50% gray. In most cases this works but when white or black is dominating it doesn't. An object against a light or dark background has no average tone of 50% gray. The camera meter will show values that underexpose or overexpose the image to make it 50% gray.

Make another experiment. Set your camera to manual exposure mode and adjust the exposure so that the gray area is correctly exposed according to your camera. Although your camera will indicate over- or underexposure keep that exposure setting when you photograph the white and the black area. This time you'll have correct images of a gray, a white and a black area.

Purchase an 18% gray card in a camera store and use it before you shoot a picture. Set your camera into manual mode and set the exposure measurement system to spot metering. Place the gray card so that is lit by the same light than the object you want to photograph. Point your camera to the gray card and adjust the exposure. If the light doesn't change you only have to do this one time and all your subsequent photos will be optimal exposed. At least they will be closer then ever to the correct exposure and very little has to be done later in Photoshop.

You don't want to always carry a gray card with you? Meter the palm of your hand instead. It is not gray but you can calibrate it by using a gray card. Adjust exposure using the gray card, then under the same light, meter the palm of your hand. The exposure will be off. Let's say it is off by +1 step. This offset will be the same in all lightning situations. From now on when you measure the exposure using the palm of your hand adjust it so that it is one step below the value the camera thinks is correct.

Use the RAW shooting mode

If your digital camera offers a RAW shooting mode use it instead of the JPEG format because it offers much more quality. You get the raw sensor data that can be modified later on your computer with much more accuracy and processing power.

Simplify your Image
Simplify the image by removing distractions either by choosing a different camera angle or if that is not possible do it later in Photoshop. Get close and don't waste pixels around your object. You can also crop the image later in Photoshop but getting close will preserve the full resolution of your image.

Choose a trim size with white paper stock
For best photo reproduction you will want white paper in your book. Note that Lightning Source uses white 50 lb. paper stock only for trim sizes of 6.14 x 9.21 inches and larger. All books with smaller trim sizes are printed on crème 55 lb. paper stock.

Sharpen extremely
Images need to be extremely sharpened to look good on a 600 dpi laser print. Look at the example below or at the original images from my book on building lap steel guitars in the *My Examples* section. Inexperienced as I was I sharpened those images just enough to look good on screen. By adjusting and sharpening them as explained in this book your images will print a lot better.

Original

Sharpened

10-step Photoshop work flow

Step 1: Clean up the image
Spot Healing Brush Tool, Healing Brush Tool, Patch Tool

Step 2: Pre-sharpen the image
FILTER > SHARPEN > SMART SHARPEN

Step 3: Remove the background (optional)
Path Tool

Step 4: Bring the picture to the required resolution and size
Crop Tool
IMAGE > IMAGE SIZE

Step 5: Adjust the image
IMAGE > ADJUSTMENTS > AUTO COLOR
IMAGE > ADJUSTMENTS > AUTO CONTRAST

Step 6: Make a grayscale photo
IMAGE > ADJUSTMENTS > CHANNEL MIXER
IMAGE > MODE > GRAYSCALE

Step 7: Increase the contrast (optional)
IMAGE > ADJUSTMENT > CURVES

Step 8: Compensate for midtone dot gain
IMAGE > ADJUSTMENT > CURVES

Step 9: Sharpen the image for 85 lpi, uncoated paper

For grayscale images:
Step 10: Convert to 8-bit, Grayscale mode and save as TIFF
IMAGE > MODE > 8-BIT
FILE > SAVE AS

For prescreened images:
Step 10: Prescreen the image and save as BMP
IMAGE > MODE > BITMAP
FILE > SAVE AS

Step 1: Clean up the image

When an image gets sharpened all blemishes will also be amplified. You don't need to be extra careful because the coarse screen doesn't show fine detail but some cleanup of dust specks and other things should be done. This is especially necessary when you have a light background. Photoshop offers the *Spot Healing Brush Tool, Healing Brush Tool* and *Patch Tool* for this task. You can also remove distracting parts of the image that would otherwise only move the eye away from the subject.

Step 2: Presharpen the image

This should only be a very light and subtle sharpening of the image. Use the *Smart Sharpen Filter* and set it to *Remove: Lens Blur* because this gives cleaner results (*Remove: Gaussian Blur* gives the same results as the good old *Unsharp Mask Filter*). Preview the image at 100% and adjust the values so that the sharpening effect is barely visible (start with 100% and a radius of 1 pixel for example). If you prefer you can also use the *High Pass Filter* sharpening technique described in step 9. Some third party sharpening software also offer a presharpening step.

Step 3: Remove the background (optional)

Removing the background is a good way to simplify an image and to reduce it to the essential part. If you have a simple object that has high contrast to the background and hard edges the *Magic Wand* tool alone may do the trick. If your object is hairy try the IMAGE > EXTRACT command and refine the result manually. For all other objects the best method is using the *Pen Tool*. It may seem tedious and it is but no other method gives you pixel accurate control of what is cut off and what remains in the final picture.

With the *Pen Tool* carefully draw a path around the object. Do this section by section at a high zoom setting. When you reach the edge press the space bar and move to the next section. Useful keyboard shortcuts are **A** to switch to the *Direct Selection Tool* just in case a point or handle has to be adjusted and **P** to return to the *Pen Tool*. When you arrive at the starting point click on it to close the path.

When your path is finished go to the *Paths* palette (WINDOW > PATHS) and choose *Make Selection* in the window fly out menu. Continue with LAYER > NEW > LAYER VIA COPY or STR/CMD + J and turn off the background layer visibility. The image on the new layer now has a transparent background. If the image was on a contrasting background before there will be some distracting background pixels that contaminate the edges. Get rid of these by using LAYER > MATTING > DEFRINGE. A one pixel width will be fine in most cases. If your object was on a black or white background there are also specific LAYER > MATTING > REMOVE BLACK MATTE or LAYER > MATTING > REMOVE WHITE MATTE commands.

The safest way to use transparency in your document is the use of the Encapsulated Postscript (EPS) format. Choose HELP > EXPORT TRANSPARENT IMAGE to save the image together with the clipping path as an EPS file that can be placed into your layout program.

Step 4: Bring the picture to the required resolution and size

Image quality and sharpness will most likely suffer if you scale photos later in the layout program. For optimum results scale pictures to the required resolution and size in Photoshop only. It's important to understand that in the IMAGE > IMAGE SIZE dialog shown below the document size is determined by the pixel dimensions and the resolution (e.g. 1200 pixels divided by 600 pixels/inch gives a width of 2 inches).

Always bring the image to the final dimensions that are required in your document. Check the *Resample Image* box and at *Document Size* enter the required resolution and then the required size. Note that the image will be altered because pixels have to be removed or added as soon as you hit *OK*. Use *Bicubic Sharper* as the calculation method when pixels have to be removed and *Bicubic Smoother* when pixels have to be added i.e. the image is enlarged.

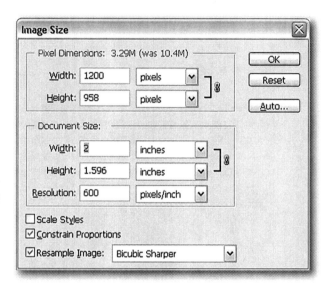

If you use grayscale TIFF files

See the examples on the facing page and decide yourself if you see any difference between a 300 ppi or a 600 ppi TIFF file. Normally 1.5 to 2 times the line screen is all you need so 300 ppi should be more then enough. In fact 300 ppi files are sufficient for any printing process including high quality 150 lpi offset printing. But there is also the user manual of the Andromeda Screens filter plugin which tells you that the pixel per inch of the picture to be screened should be *at least* four times the lines per inch for better grayscale reproduction in the screened result. I don't know if this applies also for in-printer screening. Because I used 600 ppi files for all prescreened examples in this book and I also used 600 ppi grayscale TIFF files. This extra data may be unnecessary and just thrown away in the screening process. Also an 600 ppi, 8-bit grayscale picture is four times larger in file size then a 300 ppi one.

TIFF	Images marked with "TIFF" where prepared as 8-bit grayscale images and saved in TIFF format as described above.
BMP	Images marked with "BMP" where prepared by converting an 8-bit grayscale image to a 1-bit (black & white only) prescreened bitmap and then saved as BMP files. An 85 lpi halftone screen was applied unless specified otherwise.

1809 x 1703 pixel @ 600 ppi

905 x 852 pixel @ 300 ppi

513 x 483 pixel @ 170 ppi

513 x 483 pixel @ 170 ppi
(Photokit Sharpener)

In the *image Size* dialog window is an *Auto* button that brings you to the *Auto Resolution* dialog shown on the right. After entering a line screen of 85 lpi and *Best Quality* the image is resized to 170 ppi (2 x 85). In print this is considered "best". We'll see if this applies to print on demand in the two pictures

above. All pictures on this page where sharpened with nik Sharpener Pro 2.0 except the one in the lower right corner. I used the Photokit Sharpener plugin (www.pixelgenius.com) for sharpening it because it offers a dedicated 85 lpi, 170 ppi halftone setting. The picture looks better but much less sharpened on screen.

If you use prescreened BMP files

If prescreening turns out to be the better way of publishing with Lightning Source then always use 600 ppi originals. The user manual of the Andromeda Screens filter plugin suggests that the pixel per inch of the picture to be screened should be *at least* four times the lines per inch for better grayscale reproduction in the screened result. Because there is more data to calculate the screen from grayscale simulation will look better. Prescreened 1-bit Bitmaps are line art and always must have the full printer resolution of 600 dpi. At 85 lpi the "four times the line screen" requirement is also easily met. Never ever resize a prescreened bitmap picture! It has a fixed resolution with a dedicated line screen and everything will fall apart when you change the size later in the layout program. If you decide to use a smaller or larger picture later go back to Photoshop, resize the original and then prescreen the new size again.

Step 5: Adjust the image

Before we convert the image into a grayscale image we want an image that is correctly adjusted, that virtually pops off the screen. Although the most precise correction of images is done in the *Curves* dialog the auto correction features built into Photoshop can be a great time saver. Under IMAGE > ADJUSTMENTS you'll find three auto adjustment commands. Try *Auto Color* followed by *Auto Contrast*. In most cases this will significantly improve your image but if you're not pleased with the result you can always go back to the beginning using WINDOW > HISTORY.

If you prefer a preview and/or an adjustment layer you'll find all auto adjustment commands by clicking the *Options* button in the *Levels* or *Curves* dialog.

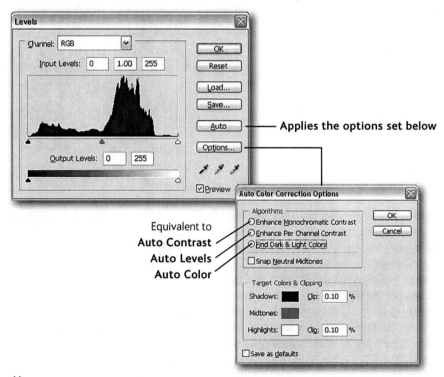

Applies the options set below

Equivalent to
Auto Contrast
Auto Levels
Auto Color

Step 6: Convert to grayscale

Before you proceed save a copy of the adjusted color photo. This copy can be processed later for use in an eBook or on a website.

Channel Mixer Method

In WINDOW > CHANNELS click on the individual RGB channels and note the ones that look good. If a channel looks bad don't use it. The mix is made by using IMAGE > ADJUSTMENTS > CHANNEL MIXER... Check the *Monochrome* check box then enter the percentage you want to use from each channel. For best results the percentage of all three channels should add up to 100%. You can also look at the Red, Green or Blue channel alone by setting just that channel to 100% (and the other two to 0%). Follow the conversion by IMAGE > MODE > GRAYSCALE as this will lower the file size without compromising quality.

The Russel Brown Technique of Converting Color to B&W

Russel Browns (www.russelbrown.com) method allows for interactive adjustment of the conversion process by creating two *Hue/Saturation Adjustment Layers*. Leave the *Blend Mode* of the top layer at *Normal* and adjust the *Saturation* in the dialog box to -100. Set the *Blend Mode* of the middle layer to *Color*. Now adjust the *Hue* and/or *Saturation* in the dialog box of the middle layer until you are pleased with the result. By selecting red, blue or green in the *Edit* box you can limit your adjustment to just that color values.

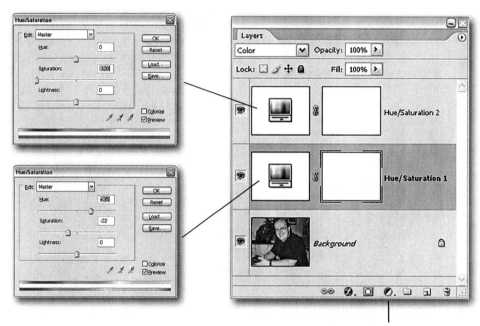

Click on this icon to create a new adjustment layer (select Hue/Saturation...)

Rob Carr Color to B&W Conversion Technique

For rich, high contrast black and white photos try a technique developed by photo retoucher Rob Carr. It requires several mode conversions so it's best to use it on 16-bit images. Because I liked the results a lot and because there is - if at all - only one slider to set (the *Fill Layer Opacity*) all examples in this book where converted by this method.

Convert to Lab Color (IMAGE > MODE > LAB COLOR)

Select the *Lightness* channel in the Channels palette

Convert to Grayscale (IMAGE > MODE > GRAYSCALE)

Select all highlights in the new *Gray* channel (Control (Mac: Command)-click the channel)

Invert the selection to select the shadows (SELECT > INVERSE)

Fill the selection with black (In LAYER > NEW FILL LAYER > SOLID COLOR... select black RGB=0)

Lower the opacity of the fill layer to 25-50% or if the image gets too dark lower it to 0%.

Step 7: Increase the contrast (optional)

Depending on the picture you may want to increase the contrast just a little bit. Do this by setting a very gentle S-curve in IMAGE > ADJUSTMENT > CURVES...

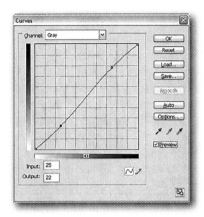

Or duplicate the *Background* layer and set the *Blend Mode* of the duplicated layer to *Soft Light*. Adjust the contrast by setting the layer opacity to 25%.

Step 8: Compensate for midtone dot gain

If you don't take dot gain into account images will print darker than displayed on screen. Dot gain usually is a problem of ink based printing where the wet paint spreads out while it dries on the paper. Dot gain mainly effects middle gray values from 40 to 60 percent. Larger dots progessively touch each other and have less perimeter available for the growth. To determine the dot gain percentage a print of 50% gray is measured with a tensiometer. If the printed gray reads 65% dot gain is 15%.

Laser printing is a dry printing process and the toner particles are fused to the top of the paper surface so there isn't any conventional midtone dot gain. But there is a similar effect because of uneven placement of toner particles and spill (the toner particles of a 50% gray halftone dot when viewed through a microscope look more like an accumulation of ground pepper). According to Lightning Source their midtone dot gain is approximately 20%.

By comparing images from my book on lap steel guitars with the appearance on screen I found the closest match in the *Gamma 2.2 Working Space*. I used a monitor calibrated to a white point of 6500K and a gamma of 2.2.

Set the *Gray* entry field to *Gray Gamma 2.2* under EDIT > COLOR SETTINGS > WORKING SPACES and grayscale images are displayed darker so you automatically adjust them correct visually. There is also a dedicated *Gray: Dot Gain 20% Working Space* but I found the *Gray Gamma 2.2 Working Space* did a much more accurate job of simulating the look in print.

If the IBM RIP does compensate for midtone dot gain and if there is dot gain the 50% gray area on the left will appear like a "18% gray" card used in photography (an "18% gray" card is actually 50% or middle gray with RGB values of 128 each).

If the IBM RIP doesn't compensate for midtone dot gain and if there is a dot gain of 20% then the 30% gray area on the left will print 20% darker as approximately 50% gray.

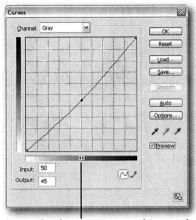 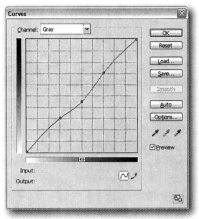

Press this button to put white to the left (this way Photoshop shows the grayscale values in percent)

Lighten midtones only

If midtones display too dark in the *Gamma 2.2 Working Space* you have to lighten them. An adjustment curve like the left one above is not ideal because it also lightens values outside the midtone range. Use such a curve if the entire picture is too dark. If you don't want to lighten the entire image but the midtones you can limit the adjustment to just the midtone values by nailing the curve down at 30 and 70 percent as shown on the right above.

Another way to lighten just midtones without fiddling with curves is to make and lighten a selection of only midtone values by using SELECT > COLOR RANGE... as shown below. The *Blend Mode* of *Screen* acts like light shining through the selection. Adjust the *Layer Opacity* to 25% or lower.

Select *Midtones*

By toggling the layer visibility you get a before and after view.

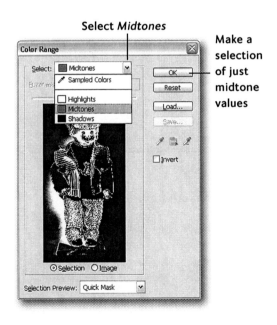

Make a selection of just midtone values

Set *Blend Mode* to *Screen*

Adjust *Opacity* to a low value.

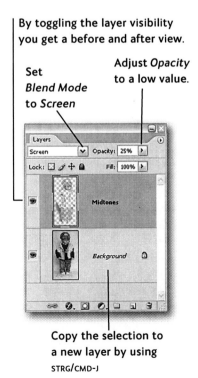

Copy the selection to a new layer by using STRG/CMD-J

49

Step 9: Sharpen the image for 85 lpi, uncoated paper

A line screen of 85 lpi requires very high, almost crazy sharpening that looks too strong when viewed at 100% size on screen. To get a better impression of the result look at such an oversharpened picture at 25% size. Unfortunately extreme sharpening also sharpens noise, grain or skin pores. To look good in print on demand you want to amplify just the edges without bringing too much grain into the rest of the pictures.

Nik Sharpener Pro (www.niksoftware.com) a quite expensive Photoshop plugin does a quick and excellent sharpening job for a lot of output devices. The software analyses every picture and automatically applies the correct sharpening amount according to your output device settings. Because pictures sharpened with this software consistently looked a bit better than my own trials I used it for almost all the examples in this book. I let you know when I used another sharpening method for a particular picture.

You can use any sharpening method you like but to get a feeling of how much sharpening has to be applied to a 85 lpi halftone screen print I recommend you download the demo version of nik Sharpener Pro. Although the demo version overlays a tiny "DEMO" print all over the sharpened image it allows for very good judgement of the sharpening result. Try to get close to this result with your own sharpening method.

For print on demand purposes I found that I could get very close to the nik Sharpener Pro results by using Photoshops *High Pass Filter* sharpening method.

High Pass sharpening method:
1 Duplicate the *Background* layer (LAYER > DUPLICATE LAYER).
2 Open FILTER > OTHER > HIGHPASS... Your picture will look gray now. Adjust the *Radius* so that only edges you want to get sharpened are visible. Hit *OK*.
3 Optional: paint away any parts you don't want to be sharpened by either using a 50% gray soft brush or by filling a selection with 50% gray.
4 Set the layer blend mode to *Soft Light*. This blend mode is a more gentle version of the *Overlay* mode and only pixels that are lighter or darker than 50% gray have an effect on the layer underneath.
5 The sharpening effect is too weak for a 85 lpi line screen therefore duplicate the layer several times till the sharpening effect gets very strong. The shortcut for duplicating a layer is CTRL+J (or COMMAND+J on a Mac).

For the two pictures at the bottom of the facing page I used a *High Pass Filter* with a *Radius* of 2.5. I copied the layer 7 times to get a sharpening result similar to that of nik Sharpener Pro.

After sharpening it is sometimes necessary to clean up from unwanted amplified spots. The best tool for this is the *Spot Healing Brush*.

If you want to sharpen just parts of an image apply the sharpening filter to a copy of the background layer. Add a layer mask, fill it with black and using a soft, white paintbrush paint over the mask where you want the sharpening to be applied to the background layer. Try the *Selective* tool of nik Sharpener Pro (can also be the demo version) to fully understand selective sharpening using layer masks.

Facing page: My brother, quite happy with his new digital camera.

Sharpened with nik Sharpener Pro
Halftone
Viewing Distance: Up to 2 feet
Printer Resolution: 85 lpi
Paper Type: Uncoated.

Sharpened by 8x High Pass filter
Radius: 2.5
Blend Mode: Soft Light

Step 10: Save the image in TIFF format

If you worked in 16-bit mode so far change to 8-bit mode using IMAGE > MODE > 8-BIT then save the image as an uncompressed *TIFF* file without layers. (*Image Compression: NONE, Pixel Order: Interleaved, Byte Order: IBM PC*).

> **Should you compress the tonal range as explained in Step 12?**
> I was told that the IBM RIP does compensate for the loss in the shadows and highlights by compressing the tonal range of an image to 10-85%. Any adjustments made by you will be adjusted again resulting in a print that is too light. The safest and best approach is to deliver 8-bit grayscale TIFF files with a tonal range of 0-100% and correct midtones when viewed in the *Gamma 2.2 Working Space*.

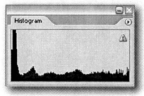

As shown in the *Histogram* above the 8-bit image of my son Tobias has 0% and 100% gray values. The 10 to 85% gray compression adjustment was applied by the IBM-RIP.

Prescreening

Why prescreening?

This is the part where some uncertainty comes in. It is an experiment. The prescreened versions of this book generally looked better and crisper on my consumer level 600 dpi laser printer than the ones that got screened by this printer. But will the prescreened 1-bit bitmap images also look better when printed on an IBM Infoprint machine? That's the question and because I don't have such a baby at my command this book is sort of a shot into the dark. I will only know when I receive my proof copy from Lightning Source.

Since my first book "Building Electric Guitars" Lightning Source has installed new IBM Infoprint machines and the grayscale quality got better. Of course there's always room to improve. I have seen the excellent printing quality of a 600 dpi Apple LaserWriter Select 360 and wouldn't even think of prescreening if print on demand would use such fine hardware. I also use the German print on demand company Book on Demand (www.bod.de) for the German versions of my books. They use Xerox machines and the grayscale photo quality is much better (I supplied them with the very same image data).

Lightning Source does an excellent job in printing line art or type so if the IBM Infoprint machine is confronted with a prescreened, 1-bit, black & white bitmap image it should print it halftone dot by halftone dot as line art. We will see. If this concept fails you can still use all of the following image preparation steps except the last ones.

Advantage of prescreening

With prescreened images you are independent of any adjustments that may be applied to grayscale images in the Raster Image Processor or printer driver software. You can use the full processing power of your desktop computer for adjusting images individually and you have complete control over the screening process by using software like the Andromeda screens plugin.

Disadvantage of prescreening

The prescreened pictures in this book will not benefit should Lightning Source switch to 1200 dpi monochrome printing one day (not likely any time soon). The picture quality will stay the same. Grayscale images on the other hand will improve automatically without the need for remastering the whole book. Although for optimal results image quality would then benefit from sharpening for the new 106 lpi line screen.

UPDATE

After seeing the first proof copy of this book I doubt that prescreening photos is worth the extra effort. The quality of the 8-bit grayscale images was (and hopefully still is) better than ever. My ten photo preparation steps give great results. In this book version I can only try to improve the prescreened versions to match this result. If the prescreened photos are not better than the grayscale ones, it doesn't make sense to prescreen (unless you want to use a different line screen and/or dot shape of course).

Alternative step 10: Prescreen the image and save it in BMP format

Prescreening during conversion to *Bitmap Mode*

Convert the image into a 1-bit black and white prescreened bitmap (IMAGE > MODE > BITMAP). You will have to flatten all layers during this process. Save the result as a *BMP* file. Note that the *Bitmap Mode* is only available if the image is in *Grayscale Mode*. To apply a 600 ppi, 85 lpi, 45° round dot halftone screen follow the screenshots below.

For optimal results use 600 ppi input data

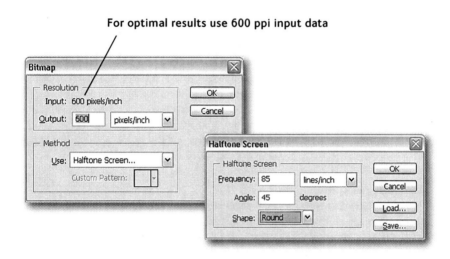

Pre-screening with the Andromeda Screens Filter plugin

Andromeda (www.andromeda.com) offers a screens filter plugin that allows more artistic screening of photos. Although when used with the settings shown below it does the same as Photoshops own screening option but with better quality. The "corrected dots" feature analyses a picture prior to screening and helps to minimize posterization.

Follow up this filter by a conversion into *Bitmap Mode* using IMAGE > MODE > BITMAP > 50% THRESHOLD. This step saves a lot of storage space without any quality loss.

The picture on the right was screened with the Andromeda Screens plugin using the settings shown above. When viewed very close on screen there really is a better, more even distribution of halftone dots visible. Will this subtle difference be visible in print on demand? Find it out by comparing it to the picture on the facing page which was prescreened using IMAGE > MODE > BITMAP.

55

What's about compressing the tonal range?

Because there are only 50 shades of gray in a 600 ppi / 85 lpi halftone screen some very light grays will appear white (the halftone dots are too fine to get printed). Also because toner dots grow together much earlier than calculated many of the very dark grayscale values will appear black. Take a look at the grayscale values below. Where do you see the first area that isn't black or white any more? On my laser printer all gray values down to 85% appeared black and the first light gray appeared at 5% (although the 5% gray was not very clean). Note this black and white clipping values. It doesn't make sense to leave grayscale values in the image that are darker or lighter than this values because the printing process can't differentiate between them (e.g. every gray values above 85% are printed black and all values below 5% are printed white). Limiting the tonal range makes sure that there are only grayscale values in the picture. For a 600 dpi laser printer it is safe to use a 10-85% tonal range.

BMP

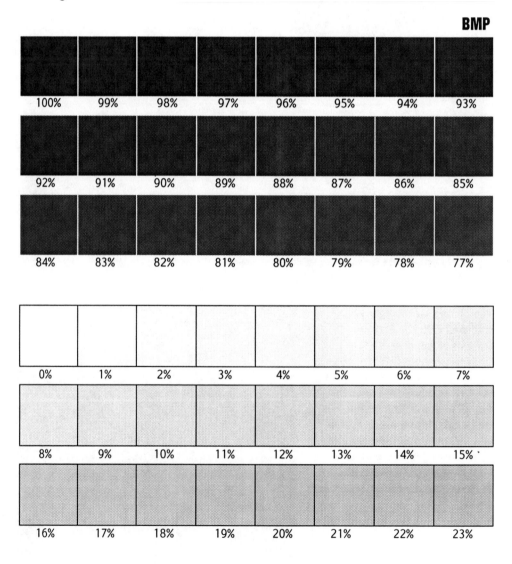

| 100% | 99% | 98% | 97% | 96% | 95% | 94% | 93% |

| 92% | 91% | 90% | 89% | 88% | 87% | 86% | 85% |

| 84% | 83% | 82% | 81% | 80% | 79% | 78% | 77% |

| 0% | 1% | 2% | 3% | 4% | 5% | 6% | 7% |

| 8% | 9% | 10% | 11% | 12% | 13% | 14% | 15% · |

| 16% | 17% | 18% | 19% | 20% | 21% | 22% | 23% |

I was told that the Raster Image Processor (RIP) in the IBM Infoprint machine does automatically compress the tonal range of grayscale images to 10-85%. (0% gray becomes 10%, 100% becomes 85% and the rest goes in between). But this doesn't apply to prescreened 1-bit bitmap images. The prescreened samples on the facing page are not effected by the RIP (they are line art) so any tonal adjustments must be applied by you.

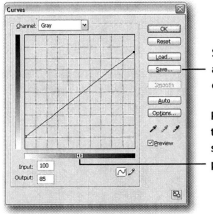

Save the adjustment curve

Press this button to put white to the left (this way Photoshop shows the grayscale values in percent)

To limit the tonal range to 10%-85% drag the lower left point up to 10% and lower the upper right point to 85%. The image looses contrast on screen but will print correctly. At least in offset printing. See the note below.

Histogram (distribution view of tonal values in an image) after compressing the tonal range.

Examine the image

Use the *Pipette Tool* together with the *Info Palette* to examine the highlights and shadows in the image. Adjusting both ends of the curve is only needed when there are gray values above 85% and below 10% in the image. You can also adjust just one end if the other end doesn't need to be compressed.

Sometimes it's difficult to find specific tonal values in an image. To find any parts with 0% gray for example set the *Foreground Color* to white in the *Color Palette* then go to SELECT > COLOR RANGE... Set the *Fuzziness* slider to zero and hit OK to see a selection of every 0% gray area in the image.

SO FAR THE THEORY

In practise however limiting the tonal range of prescreened pictures to 10%-85% did degrade contrast. In a previous proof copy of this book all prescreened images had no contrast and appeared flat. The reason can be seen on the facing page: 85% gray doesn't print black on the IBM Infoprint machine. Therefore I didn't use the IMAGE > ADJUSTMENTS > CURVES dialog to limit the tonal range as shown in the screen shot above. The prescreened photos in this book have a tonal range of 0%-100%. I didn't take care of any clipping values.

Frame your picture

A thin black frame around your image will not only cover the rough edge of the coarse screen but also let the image appear sharper.

BMP

Because of the rough border the line screen becomes more appearent

By adding a black 0.75 point frame the coarse edge gets covered

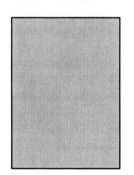 

A thicker 1 point frame

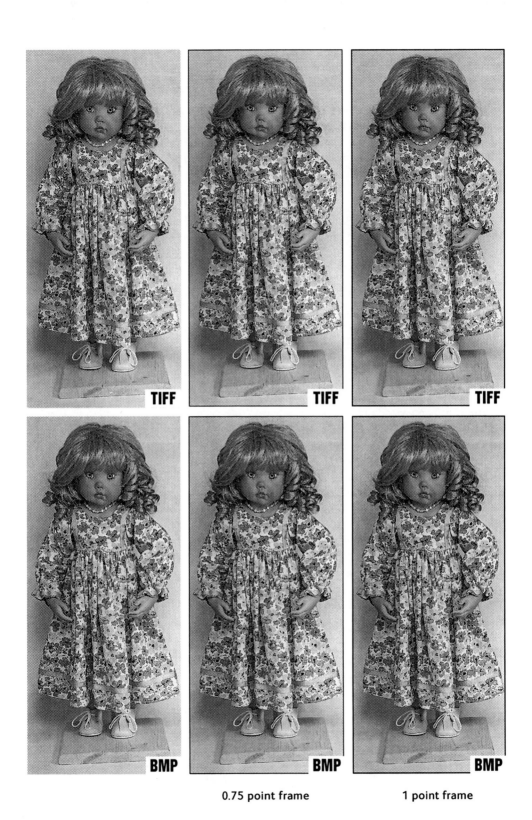

0.75 point frame   1 point frame

Stock image examples

Images on the following pages where prepared using steps 2 and 4-10 of the Photoshop work flow described earlier. The images where adjusted to look good on a calibrated monitor (6500K, Gamma 2.2) in the *Gamma 2.2 Working Space*. I used the Carr Color to B&W Conversion Method. Sharpening was applied by nik Sharpener Pro. All steps can be automated by recording them as a Photoshop *Action* (WINDOW > ACTIONS). Add stops and dialogs as appropriate.

The steps in detail:

IMAGE > MODE > 16-BIT

FILTER > SHARPEN > SMART SHARPEN
> Amount: 100%
> Radius: 1.0 pixels
> Remove: Lens Blur

IMAGE > IMAGE SIZE > 300 ppi for TIFF / 600 ppi for BMP

IMAGE > ADJUSTMENTS > AUTO COLOR

IMAGE > ADJUSTMENTS > AUTO CONTRAST

IMAGE > MODE > LAB COLOR

Select the *Lightness* channel

IMAGE > MODE > GRAYSCALE

Control-click (or on a Mac: Command-click) the new *Gray* channel

SELECT > INVERSE

LAYER > NEW FILL LAYER > SOLID COLOR... > black (RGB=0)

Set the *Fill Layer* opacity to 25-50%

LAYER > FLATTEN IMAGE

IMAGE > ADJUSTMENT > CURVES (subtle S-curve for more contrast)

FILTER > SHARPEN > NIK SHARPENER PRO > HALFTONE... (or method with similar result)
> Setting: Halftone
> Viewing distance: Up to 2 feet
> Paper type: Uncoated
> Printer resolution: 85 lpi

TIF images only:

FILE > SAVE AS TIFF

BMP images only:

IMAGE > MODE > 8-BIT

IMAGE > MODE > BITMAP
> 600 ppi
> Halftone screen
> 85 lines/inch, 45 degrees, round dot

FILE > SAVE AS BMP

TIFF Images marked with TIFF are 8-bit grayscale images with 300 ppi resolution.

BMP Images marked with BMP are 1-bit bitmap images with 600 ppi resolution.
A 85 lpi 45° round dot line screen has been applied.

Brazilian girl - Royalty free photo #555152 from www.sxc.hu
Fish - Royalty free photo #567547 from www.sxc.hu

TIFF

Old city of Dubrovnic, Croatia - Royalty free photo #578665 from www.sxc.hu

TIFF

TIFF

Statue - Royalty free photo #501952 from www.sxc.hu
Car - Royalty free photo #550716 from www.sxc.hu

Original as downloaded from www.sxc.hu

TIFF

TIFF

BMP

Church - Royalty free photo #573119 from www.sxc.hu
Horse - Royalty free photo #550437 from www.sxc.hu
Carving - Royalty free photo #501953 from www.sxc.hu

My Examples

TIFF

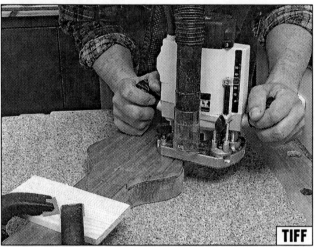

TIFF

BMP

Top images are 300 ppi grayscale images as used in my book *Build Your Own Lap Steel Guitar*. Unfortunately I only sharpened them to look good on screen. The middle and bottom images are my new attempt.

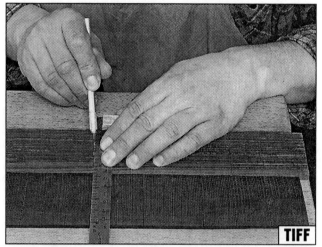

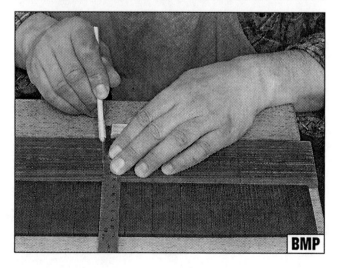

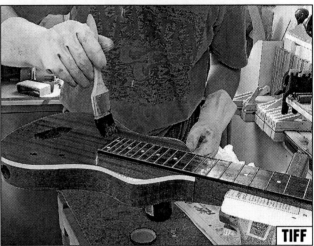

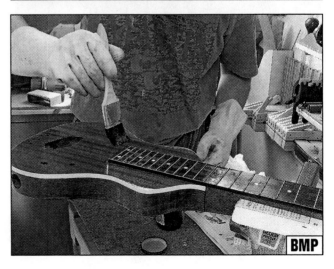

Grayscale image 300 ppi (3.4 MB)

BMP

Bitmap image 600 ppi / 85 lpi (1.7 MB)

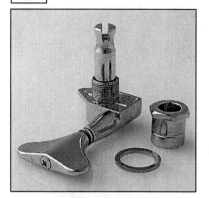

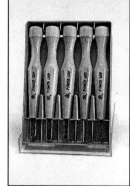

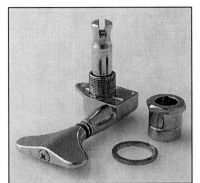

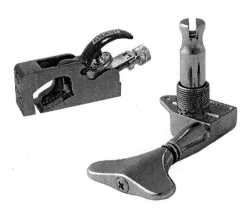

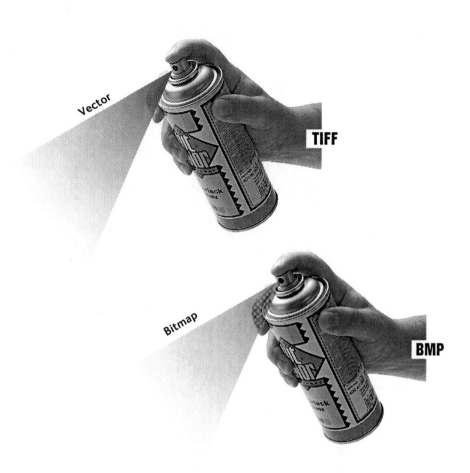

Vector

TIFF

Bitmap

BMP

This image was saved with a clipping path in EPS format (HELP > EXPORT TRANSPARENT IMAGE). This clipping path was then used for the text wrap shape.

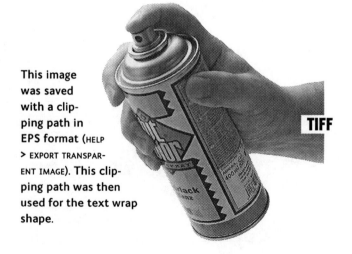

TIFF

Extreme sharpening was applied to the images on this page
before they got prescreened.
Unsharp Mask:
Amount: 500%
Radius: 5 pixels

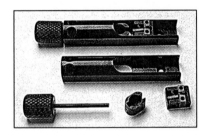

ANANT TOOLS

TIFF

300 ppi (7.3 MB)

600 ppi / 85 lpi (1.8 MB)

BMP

Large pictures with little detail like this can benefit from a coarser 65 lpi screen that allows for a softer look with about 82 possible shades of gray.

Prescreened with the Andromeda Screens filter. According to Andromeda the filters "corrected dots" should optimize grayscale distribution. An additional *Unsharp Mask* and a lower threshold where applied as shown in the screenshot below.

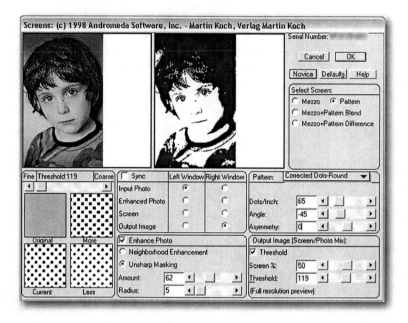

Facing page: My daughter Anna at the age of five.

600 ppi / 65 lpi

Other useful things to know

Half inch border
Because of the huge printing volume Lightning Source print on demand has to be a highly automated process. Basic quality control checks the alignment of the content of each individual page by watching the page borders. If there is content found within a 1/2 inch border around each page (I marked this border on this page) the situation has to be judged. Is it an alignment error or was the content placed intentionally? This slows down the printing of your book therefore it is best to put no contents at all closer than 1/2 inch to the cut edge. According to the premedia team of Lightning Source you can place page numbers outside this border as long as they are no closer than 1/4" to the cut edge. Because the allowed production tolerances in binding and cutting are 1/16" a page number that is closer to the edge could theoretically end up sitting right on top of the cut if both binding and trimming are off in the same direction.

No guaranteed page bleed
Lightning Source doesn't guarantee bleed off on any of the sides of each page. Let's say you want to fill a complete page with a low opacity grayscale background then you would make the image larger than the page by 1/8 inch all around so that the page is covered in all circumstances. But because the book file generation process doesn't allow to set page bleeds the art work is trimmed to the trim size and there's no room for error any longer. Bleed is only allowed on book covers.

Submit grayscale content only
Interior content should be submitted as grayscale only. No CMYK or RGB files should be submitted as input.

Color content
In Fall 2006 Lightning Source starts to offer color printing as an option. Unfortunately every single page of a book must be printed on the color machine and the ten times higher page price has to be paid for each and every page even when the particular page content is black and white. You can't mix color and black and white pages as it is possible with the German BOD company (www.bod.de). There, putting just one to ten color pages into the book increases the book price just slightly because you pay the higher price only for the color page(s) while the rest of the book is printed conventionally.

─── **This border line should be 1/2" (+/- 1/16" tolerance) from the paper edge.**

PDF-Generation

You can send a Postscript file, an original layout program file or a PDF file to most print on demand printers. The first option has the disadvantage that you have no preview of the result and the second option requires supplying all fonts used in the document. Additionally there is so much that could go wrong with such a fragile thing as an original layout program file. Who guarantees that it opens up the same in a different environment. The best and most robust delivering format is a PDF file. You not only can see a preview of all pages, you also don't have to care about fonts if you embed them correctly.

A lot of software save or exports to the PDF format today and there are also alternatives to the expensive Adobe Acrobat software available. Although the Acrobat software also offers easy printing directly to PDF it is more reliable and therefore recommended to use the Distiller software which is part of Adobe Acrobat Professional. Generating PDF files via Acrobat Distiller is a two step process. First a Postscript file is generated then this Postscript file is converted (diststilled) to the final PDF file using Distiller.

Lightning Source offers detailed settings for important publishing software and Distiller versions on their website.

Step 1: Printing a Postscript file

The Postscript file is generated by printing. In the print dialog (FILE > PRINT) choose: *Printer: Postscript® File* and *PPD: Adobe PDF* (Adobe Acrobat installs this printer and PPD) and set the options according to the detailed descriptions offered at the Lightning Source website. Note that a line screen of 85 lpi is used regardless of the screening setting in the print option dialog.

Save the settings as a print preset. I named it "LSI Text". By the way this print preset can be used for any trim size because the book pages are output centred on a Letter sized page. If you get a warning about missing links go back and fix it. If your publishing software offers a preflight step use it before printing.

Step 2: Distilling the Postscript file

Open the Distiller software and set the options according to the detailed descriptions offered by Lightning Source. Save the settings as a preset. I named it "LSI". This preset can also be used for the cover. Because there is one grayscale image with 600 ppi, I had to temporarily set *Images > Grayscale Images > Downsampling > Off* for distilling the interior.

Double click the Postscript file or drag and drop it to the Distiller window. The PDF generation starts and the PDF file is stored in the same directory as the Postscript file by default. The most important thing you should check in the finished PDF file is proper font embedding. Open it in Acrobat or Adobe Reader and look under FILE > DOCUMENT PROPERTIES > FONTS if there is an entry beneath each font listing saying "Embedded or Embedded Subset". If it is missing the font was not properly embedded.

I named the interior PDF file for this book "9783901314131txt.pdf" according to the Lightning Source file naming conventions (ISBNtxt.pdf)

How I prepared the cover of this book

I used Adobe InDesign for laying out the cover. The front cover is most important so I start with it. I open a new InDesign document (FILE > NEW) and enter the *Page Size* of this book (6.14 X 9.21 inches), *Margins* and *Bleed* as shown below.

Save your entries as a preset

Turn off
*Facing
Pages*

Press this button to
see the *Bleed* option
below

Press this button
enter *1/8* in one of
the *Margins* entry
fields and press the
TAB key. This margin
helps to keep any-
thing important 1/8
inch away from the
cut edge

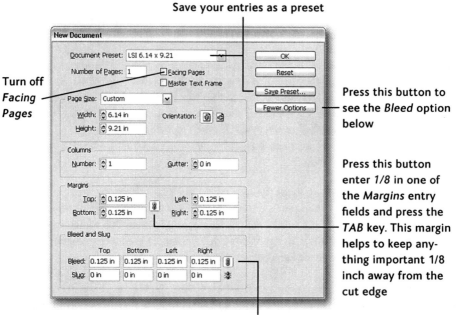

Press this button, enter *1/8* into one of the
Bleed entry fields and press the *TAB* key.

After hitting *OK* a blank page with a red bleed border appears. I want some images to bleed off the page so I make sure they extend over the page border right to the bleed border. This gives 1/8 inch room for any binding and cutting error and makes sure that the images always go right to the edge(s).

When I'm pleased with the result I mark everything and group it together and save a copy of the front cover page (FILE > SAVE A COPY). This copy can be used for making a cover image for a website for example.

The cover is printed on a 1200 dpi color printer. The line screen is 106 lpi. Photo quality is very good so there is no need to try prescreening. Sharpen cover photos for 106 lpi, *coated* paper. All color and all images must be in CMYK Mode. Black should be 60c 40m 40y 100k.
The cover PDF or TIFF should contain the back cover, the spine (Lightning Source offers a spine width calculator at their website) and the front cover.

To add the back cover I double the page width in the FILE > DOCUMENT SETUP... dialog.

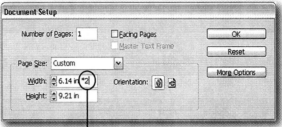

You can perform calculations in the entry fields of Adobe programs:
Add *2 then press the TAB key to double the page width to 12.28 inches.

The column guide line divides the cover
into the front and back cover area

Then I add two columns with a Gutter of *0* in the LAYOUT > MARGINS AND COLUMNS... dialog box as shown above. I move the grouped cover artwork back to the original position and add the back cover contents. I also make sure to have a 3" wide by 2" high blank area in one of the bottom back cover corners for the bar code that will be added by Lightning Source. When finished I group the content of the back cover.

To add the spine I go to www.lightningsource.com. Under Resources > Book Designers' Resources there is a Spine Calculation link that brings you to the Lightning Spine Width Calculator. After entering the page count of 84 (the book had 84 pages when I wrote this) and the book type of *Big Perfect (larger than 6.0 X 9.0)* I get a result of 0.174 inches. This spine width must be added to the document as shown below.

I add +0.174 and press the TAB key to add
the calculated spine width to the document

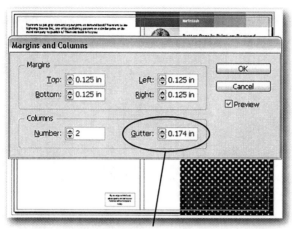

To see the spine I add a gutter of 0.174 inches between the two columns

On covers of English books the text of the spine runs from top to bottom i.e. it has to be rotated by -90 degrees. The spine usually contains the name of the author and the book title. This book is very thin so the spine is very narrow. In fact 80 pages is the limit for adding spine text. Books with less than 80 pages can't have text on the spine. Because the spine text is quite small (8.5 points) I set the title in capital letters. After zooming in I centre the spine text between the spine guide lines by eye.

Making the PDF file

For best results deliver the cover also in PDF format because type will print with higher quality compared to delivering a TIFF file The PDF file should be generated just like the one for the interior by printing to a Postscript file that is then distilled into a PDF file.

The most important settings in the printing dialog are:

Setup > Paper Size: Custom: The width entry field shows a value that equals twice the book width plus the spine width.

Marks and Bleed > Bleed and Slug: Check *Use Document Bleed Settings.* If you go back to the width entry field you will see that two times the bleed of 1/8" was added to the width and height values.

Output > Color > Composite CMYK

Download the *Cover PostScript/PDF Settings* instructions from www.lightningsource.com to see how the rest has to be set. I saved the settings as a Print Preset and named it "LSI Cover".

The Distiller settings are the same as for the interior content.

I named the cover PDF file "9783901314131cvr.pdf" according to the Lightning Source file naming conventions (ISBNcvr.pdf)

CMYK values of the colors on the back cover

	A	B	C	D	E	F	G	H	I	J
1	0c 0m 0y 100k	0c 0m 0y 90k	0c 0m 0y 80k	0c 0m 0y 70k	0c 0m 0y 60k	0c 0m 0y 50k	0c 0m 0y 40k	0c 0m 0y 30k	0c 0m 0y 20k	0c 0m 0y 10k
2	60c 40m 40y 100k	10c 100m 100y 10k	10c 100m 100y 0k	0c 70m 100y 0k	0c 40m 100y 0k	0c 20m 100y 0k	0c 0m 100y 0k	100c 0m 100y 30k	70c 0m 100y 0k	30c 0m 60y 0k
3	90c 40m 0y 0k	70c 20m 0y 0k	50c 0m 10y 0k	100c 70m 0y 0k	70c 70m 0y 0k	50c 50m 0y 0k	30c 30m 0y 0k	20c 40m 50y 20k	40c 80m 90y 20k	10c 80m 80y 20k
4	10c 80m 90y 10k	10c 50m 80y 10k	10c 80m 60y 0k	60c 30m 30y 40k	60c 30m 50y 40k	60c 30m 70y 40k	60c 60m 80y 40k	30c 40m 50y 40k	50c 20m 50y 60k	0c 70m 40y 40k
5	0c 10m 40y 60k	20c 40m 70y 0k	20c 0m 10y 20k	10c 20m 60y 0k	60c 100m 100y 40k	30c 30m 60y 40k	60c 10m 30y 40k	40c 70m 40y 30k	0c 60m 60y 30k	60c 80m 80y 10k
6	30c 60m 50y 0k	40c 60m 70y 10k	60c 60m 50y 10k	50c 50m 50y 0k	0c 40m 20y 0k	10c 50m 30y 0k	40c 30m 30y 0k	50c 40m 40y 0k	0c 30m 40y 0k	30c 60m 80y 30k
7	40c 40m 60y 40k	50c 60m 50y 30k	100c 40m 0y 0k	0c 15m 50y 10k	20c 40m 70y 0k	90c 60m 50y 40k	60c 100m 60y 40k	70c 10m 0y 0k	40c 50m 40y 40k	100c 0m 0y 0k
8	60c 0m 60y 60k	0c 50m 100y 0k	0c 70m 10y 0k	70c 0m 40y 0k	0c 30m 100y 0k	12c 46m 100y 0k	62c 45m 3y 0k	13c 93m 100y 3k	45c 5m 77y 0k	29c 45m 0y 0k
9	0c 50m 80y 0k	0c 30m 50y 0k	20c 50m 10y 0k	10c 0m 0y 20k	30c 100m 10y 0k	0c 60m 60y 0k	70c 0m 50y 0k	60c 0m 50y 90k	10c 80m 80y 10k	20c 40m 80y 0k
10	10c 70m 80y 10k	70c 70m 10y 0k	70c 70m 60y 40k	40c 90m 80y 20k	0c 10m 50y 10k	30c 30m 40y 30k	0c 100m 30y 0k	10c 0m 20y 0k	0c 50m 60y 30k	0c 50m 70y 0k

To be continued at www.buildyourguitar.com/bettergray/ ...

Printed in the United States
76906LV00002B/148-150